KOOS

couture
collage

inspiration
&
techniques

Linda Chang Teufel
Foreword by Koos van den Akker

FIRST U.S. edition
published in 2002

© 2002
Linda Chang Teufel

Publisher's Cataloging
in Publication Data
Teufel, Linda Chang
Koos Couture Collage:
Inspiration & Techniques
1. Sewing
2. Quilting
I. Title
Library of Congress
Catalog Card Number:
2002 190368
ISBN# 0-9641201-7-8

10 9 8 7 6 5 4 3 2 1

Printed in Thailand

DRAGON THREADS
490 Tucker Drive
Worthington, OH 43085
www.dragonthreads.com

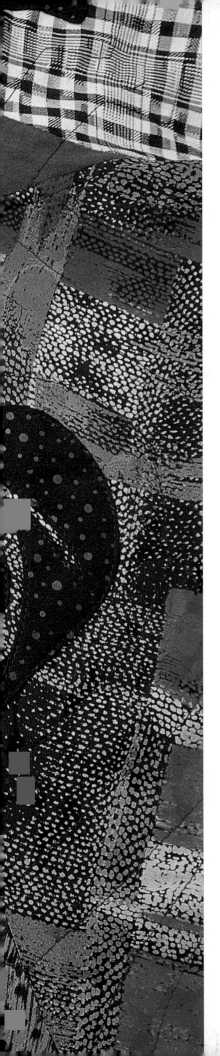

inspiration

techniques

contents

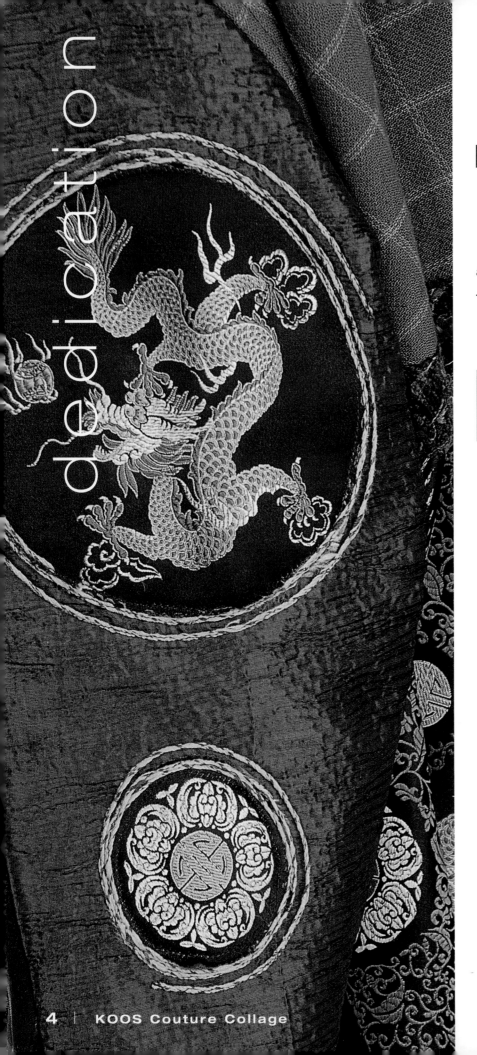

dedication

To the three most important people in my life:

my husband, Rainer

and my sons, Stefan and Anton.

Thanks for a wonderful journey!

A special dedication
to my biggest fan:
Jean B. Lange

Many sincere thanks to everyone who contributed to this book.

First of all to Koos for his generosity of time, advice and spirit. It has been so enjoyable working together again.

And to all of his great support team: Veronica Vickers, Korby Britton, Puck Meunier, Javier Valencia and Julio Cesar Barbosa.

The beauty of this book is due to the brilliant work of graphic designer and friend, Kimberly Koloski, the photography of Larry Friar and our model, Kathleen Scully.

Much appreciation to all the suppliers who generously gave their quality products to help demonstrate techniques to the reader. They are all listed in Resources (page 108).

Special thanks to Kings Road and Pat Smith for their support of this book and for the beautiful fabric lines they create for Koos.

I want to thank the family of the late Catherine Stout for their generosity with her vintage Koos couture garments.

Thank you to Harold Koda and Diahann Carroll for their very eloquent words on the work of Koos.

Finally, I am grateful to my editors, Becky Frazier, Sharyn Schnepel, Louise Cynkus and Laura Aronson.

Certain fashion designers have a signature so sharply defined that their work has a surprising quality of immutability. Even as they are constantly evolving, designers with such arresting styles develop reputations resistant to the more ephemeral aspects of fashionability and appear to exist beyond fashion itself. Like the best practitioners of the other arts, their work, while linked inevitably to their culture and historical moment, is resolutely independent in the character of its expression. Koos van den Akker with his consistent vision and idiosyncratic voice has created such a body of work, at once timely, yet timeless.

From the beginning of his career, van den Akker has explored the notion of the body as a canvas for pictorial effects. His earliest work, the virtuoso juxtaposition of textiles of varied patterns and textures that has become the great identifying mark of his oeuvre, was at first defined by the boundaries established by his fitting seams, underscoring van den Akker's reverence for tailoring and draping traditions. Very quickly, however, he broke free from the delimited fields established by conventional pattern pieces and jettisoned any notion of the symmetrical disposition of his textile mixes. He was freed, in part, by the incorporation of the appliqué technique to extend the possibilities of his surprising conjunctions of contrasting printed and textured pattern pieces. Van den Akker's lushest effects were thereafter the result of an accretion of materials, some surprisingly mundane, some breathtakingly sumptuous, but all rich in visual and tactile appeal.

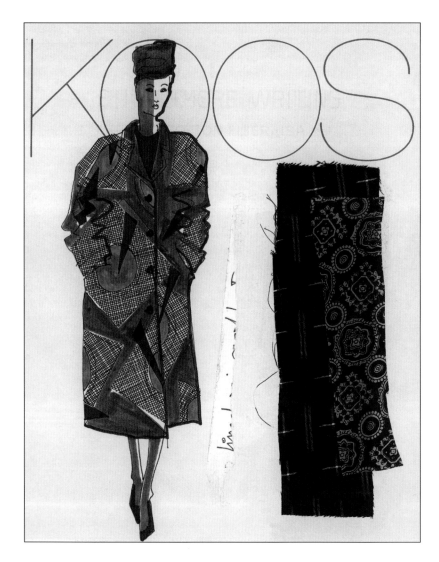

Van den Akker, as everyone will describe, is a collagist as much as a designer of apparel. But the obvious, though generally unstated, fact is that his pictorial effects are conceived and applied to an inherently three-dimensional form. Any single view of a van den Akker work is necessarily only a partial one. His designs complete themselves in motion, for it is only in a full 360 degree view that his applied compositions can fully be comprehended.

Inherent in his work is a sense of celebration of artisanal and textile traditions. From simple homespun wools to the most elaborate metallic-shot silk brocades, his arrangement of pieces and panels of fabric, while composed and coherent in the ensemble, nonetheless accentuates the distinction of each swatch. In this way, his work differs from the final effect of a collage where the separate components tend to be subordinated to an overall narrative or pictorial structure. Often, the distinction of each precious element is outlined by narrow ribbons or bindings, underscoring their visual integrity.

Inherent in his work is a sense of celebration of artisanal and textile traditions.

Formalist descriptions of his works associate him more with the intentions of early 20th century avant garde movements than to the methods of his peers in the fashion world. Therefore it is perhaps inevitable that his loyal coterie of clients collects each van den Akker design as a work of art.

Harold Koda

Curator, The Costume Institute
Metropolitan Museum of Art,
New York City

May 2002

foreword

The idea is to paint with fabric, letting the imagination fly—there really are no rules…

As I think about couture collage, I realize that this book comes at a very good time. There is a new interest and energy across America in the craft of collage. For over thirty years I've been sewing clothes for women and men, and items for the home, which begin with a very simple idea, and that is my love of fabric. I use fabric as a painter uses oils or watercolors— my palette is restricted only by the choices I make in fabric.

As a boy growing up in Holland during the war, we didn't have enough of many things including fabric. I started to make dresses out of crepe paper and later cut up a sheet to create my first *real* dress for my sister. Maybe that's why now, as I look to the incredible fabric sources available to me in New York, I feel blessed. I love having a library of fabric, an entire wall in my workroom, which I collect from unusual sources, including vintage shows, flea markets and international fabric houses. This city is one big collage, and I love reflecting its diversity, density and dynamism in my creations. My work is a marriage of pure couture workmanship and sheer fantasy. I love the extravagant and the unexpected. Using interesting textures—luxurious lace, rare leathers, furs, silks and cottons, inspires me.

Fall '88

**M**y designs come from inside; it's impulsive. I have no control over it. I don't perfect it, I just do it. But there is an interesting story. A friend gave me a beautiful book a while ago about Dutch costumes, which I never saw when I was a child. I come from a strict bourgeois background—of conservative parents— and it was wartime, so the folkloric side of Dutch culture was not part of my education. But there it all was in this book, the whole thing, the stripes against flowers—lace, leather, beautiful combinations—it gives me goose bumps, even now, to think about it. It's not that I'm interested in the old costumes, although they are exquisite. I saw so many references, such layering, such color and detail that I couldn't help but be amazed. So, this is where my signature comes from— it's almost as if what I do is subconscious, part of a heritage, yet I'm not at all a folkloric designer. I find some of the new high tech fibers and fabrics exciting and gorgeous to work with and I juxtapose old and new quite happily. There's no label that fits, what I do is original, almost organic. Not fashion, not art—just inspired, modern collage with a lot of details.

I'm constantly inventing. For instance, I like to pull yarn out of fabric and braid it, to cut leather to make lace, to knit with chiffon, and use it as piping. Tapes are always interesting—for years, I've used snaps on tape as closures for jackets and bias tape to define collaged edges. The idea is to paint with fabric, letting the imagination fly—there really are no rules, but I think that the techniques in this book should be very helpful. The home sewing industry is one which I heartily endorse, as it allows women and men to express themselves with fabric—free from fashion's constraints.

I would like to thank Linda Teufel at Dragon Threads for putting my ideas into book form. I would also like to thank Kings Road Fabrics, Vogue patterns, and Babylock sewing machines for their support of my vision. I should also mention how grateful I am to QVC for the amazing outreach of national television, making my Koos of course! line a best seller.

And last, but most importantly, thanks to my business partner, Veronica Vickers.

Koos van den Akker

June 2002

Koos's mother (right)

Koos had the innovative, forward, exciting style that I had been searching for.

As a fashion design student in New York City, I was searching for great style and design to emulate. Every season the "hot" designer collection became my favorite. Then came junior year when we had to find an apprenticeship with one of the designers or manufacturers.

I had been seeing Koos's dresses in ads and was fascinated with how beautifully and effectively he mixed patterns, colors and different textures of fabrics to create such luxurious garments. It was something totally innovative and breathtaking! I discovered that the other designers were too conservative for me with the line of their garments and traditional use of fabrics and colors. Koos had the innovative, forward, exciting style that I had been searching for. And through all these years and all the trends, I still get excited over his designs.

The man himself is a true artist. His dedication is something to respect and admire. He works long hours at his table and sewing machine. First he'll take a base garment and then he'll just roll a bolt of fabric on top of it and intuitively cut out shapes with no diagrams or pre-thoughts.

My intent for writing this book is to teach the home sewer some techniques of collage quilting and to show Koos's style as inspiration. It is also to pay tribute to a talented designer and document his work.

I am extremely grateful to Koos for all the early training, the much needed employment and friendship throughout the years. He and his staff have been more than generous and gracious with their help on this book.

Linda Chang Teufel

May 2002

It was something totally innovative and breathtaking!

KOOS

KOOS VAN DEN AKKER COUTURE, INC. 34 EAST 67TH STREET, NEW YORK, N.Y. 10021, TELEPHONE (212) 249-5432

HOTEL
GRITTI PALACE
VENEZIA

CIGA
HOTELS

Venezia May 11.

Good morning to
all

No news Good r
Still beautiful
weather and g
spirits
Hope all is we
home land ?
last day in
Tomorrow
I dreamt
last my'
and Did
the Wor
vemen*
Hope it is now....
Happy Birdsday
Sue's Mother!
For all of you
work hard!
love
KOOS.

CIAO
Jolanda
BACI
DI
VENEZIA

30124 Venezia/Telegr.: Palace Venezia/Telex: 410125 Gritti I/Telefax: 041/5250942/Tel. 041/5205166

insp

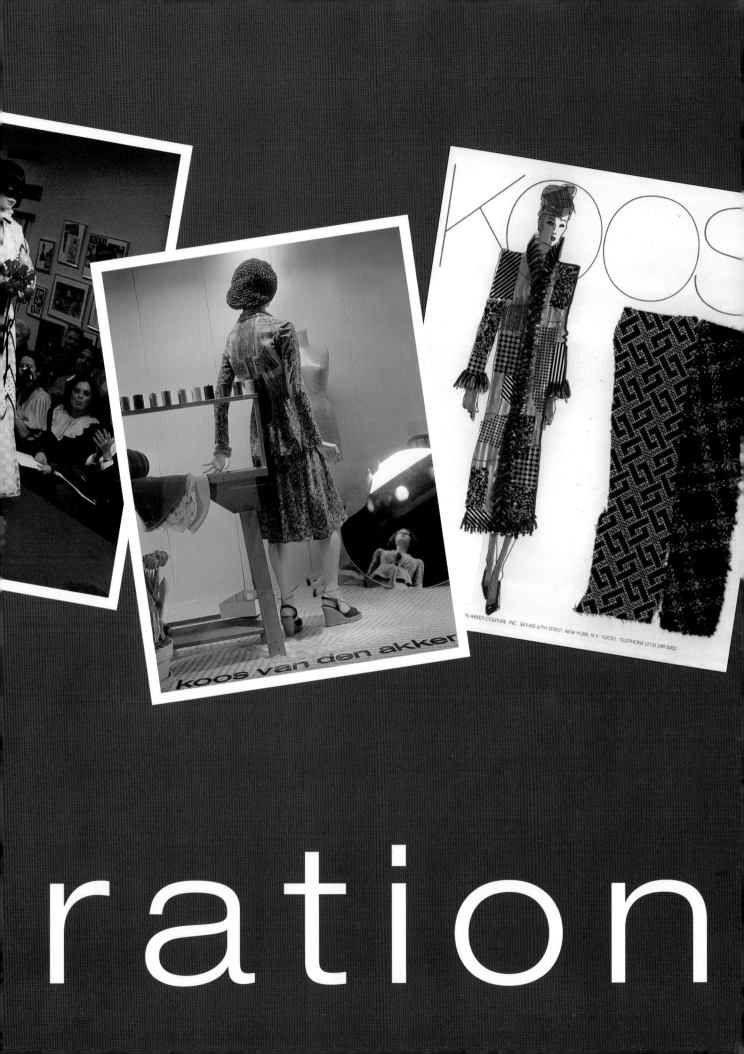

ration

biography

Koos van den Akker was born on March 16, 1939 in The Hague, Netherlands, the youngest of three children. His parents were simple, God-fearing folk who expected their son to learn a craft. In the lean years of post-war Holland, eleven-year old Koos showed his creative spirit by making clothes. His first project was a dress he made for his sister from a white bed sheet, which he embroidered with fake pearls unstrung from his mother's necklace. He taught himself to use the simple sewing machine at home and moved onto using drapes as fabric. His parents were surprised but supportive.

A wealthy uncle, who owned a beautiful house in the Dutch countryside, provided Koos with glimpses of sophistication. The uncle's grand piano introduced Koos to music, and the large garden inspired him to paint flowers. Recognizing immediately Koos's talent, his uncle arranged for the boy to go to the Royal Art School to learn to paint. The admissions committee, impressed with Koos's portfolio, allowed him to enroll at age 15, bypassing the usual requirements of age (18 years) and a high school diploma.

The first dress.

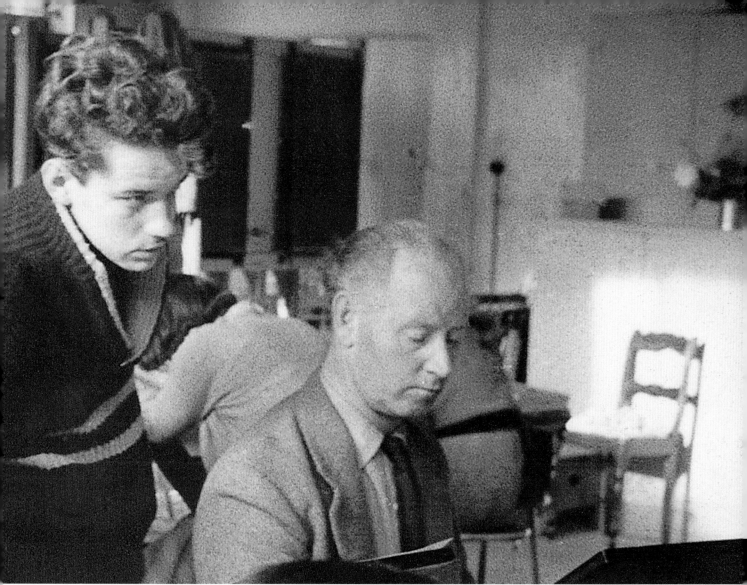

Koos in art class.

His first dress was made for his sister from a bed sheet, which he embroidered with fake pearls unstrung from his mother's necklace.

At first Koos studied fine arts, but he soon switched to the fashion department. During school holidays, Koos worked in a department store creating window displays, while making clothes for friends at night.

At age 18, Koos left art school when the army called him to fulfill his two year military obligation. When called, Koos was in the middle of sewing dresses for a wedding party so he packed them in his suitcase and took his portable sewing machine to the military base. This was something quite unusual, but was soon accepted by the other soldiers. A high-ranking officer heard about Koos's work and arranged for him to set up a workshop in a basement, where Koos made clothes for the officer's wife and daughters.

After two years in the army, Koos went to Paris. Through a recommendation from the Dutch department store, he started doing window displays for the famous Galleries Lafayette. Realizing that he needed more formal training, in 1961 he enrolled in L'Ecole Guerre Lavigne, which was located in the same building as the Christian Dior workrooms. Every year Dior offered the most gifted students an apprenticeship and in 1963, Koos was selected.

Right: Window display

COLORAMA | invitatie voor een kleurrijker leven

The first salon in the Hague.

Koos's early designs were chic and theatrical—influenced by American movies and Audrey Hepburn

Joining the Dior workroom was **the** formative learning experience for Koos. It was here that he came to understand the finer points and technicalities of sewing. This job was totally without glamour. For example, a haute couture apprenticeship required that day after day, he practice and master one special procedure—buttonholes or collars or sewing in sleeves by hand. The focus was on handwork and fit.

The job at Dior paid very little, so as usual, Koos continued to sew for customers at night in his apartment. His clientele got Dior quality at a fraction of the cost.

Koos describes his fashion today as "new couture."

"For me, new couture is not about exact fit but about embellishment of fabrics—braiding, slicing and workmanship—not tailoring. Traditional haute couture is about the body and the perfect fit of the garment. I'd rather work at my sewing machine, deriving my inspiration from the fabric. My techniques are detail oriented, so to that extent, I owe a lot to my Dior training. But, I prefer to use fabric as my palette."

After three years at Dior, and learning every detail about creating beautiful clothes, Koos returned to Holland to start his own business. Upon his return, Koos's father gave him his small savings to open a store.

In 1965, Koos opened his first salon in The Hague where he slept in a small room in the back. His extravagant window displays drew crowds of delighted design students as well as shoppers. Early designs were chic and theatrical, influenced by American movies such as "Carousel" and Audrey Hepburn as dressed by Givenchy.

But Holland was not ready for Koos—Dutch women seemed disinterested in anything glamorous or fashionable.

After the death of his father, in 1968, Koos decided to leave Holland. He wanted to go to the United States, but was told by the immigration service that America needed doctors, nurses and missionaries, not designers. So with as little delay as possible, Koos departed on a missionary's visa! The five-day Atlantic crossing gave Koos the reflective time he needed. He was fully aware that his life was about to change.

New York always held a particular fascination for Koos, ever since he first saw Hepburn in *Breakfast at Tiffany's*. The theatre, the skyline—and certainly the freedom and unlimited possibilities—spoke to the young, idealistic designer. His first stop was the top of the Empire State Building. Exhilarated and independent, Koos looked over the city and knew he was home. He would not return to Holland for 13 years.

biography (con't)

In New York, Koos set up his portable sewing machine on his hotel room bed. As he discovered New York, the fountain at Lincoln Center became a favorite meeting place; he made friends and those friends' sisters became his first customers. With only $180 to his name, he bought fabric from Macy's at $3, then sewed dresses overnight to sell at $30. Business was steadily growing.

His Lincoln Center customers followed him to his first apartment on the Upper West Side before he opened a little store on Columbus Avenue. It was one of the first stores on Columbus Avenue and soon the neighborhood came to shop.

The major turning point in Koos's career came when he opened a store on Madison Avenue and 68th Street. This is where his career really started and business flourished there for fifteen years. In the mid-70's, he started a wholesale line with a showroom at 550 Seventh Avenue, where most of the major designers had showrooms. There, and with three floors of workrooms employing 90 people, he supplied the buyers at all the major upscale stores including Bonwit Teller, Saks Fifth Avenue, Marshall Fields, Bloomingdale's and Frost Brothers.

The Columbus Avenue boutique.

Left: The Hague Salon

Koos went West in 1978 and opened a boutique on Camden Drive in Beverly Hills, with mixed results. Hollywood liked Koos's designs, but also expected the designer to be part of "the scene." It was awkward for him to maintain a high-profile L.A. life-style, while creating designs in New York at the same time. However, he established a visibility in Los Angeles, which would serve him well in the future. Entertainers were calling—Julie and Harry Belafonte, Cher, Elizabeth Taylor, Diahann Carroll, Bill Cosby and Barbara Walters all wanted Koos.

Koos won the Gold Coast Award in 1978. In 1983, the American Printed Fabrics Council gave Koos a "Tommy" award. This was also the year Koos became a United States citizen—one of his proudest moments. Fashion model Carol Alt hosted a party for him at Studio 54. Tina Sinatra, Michael & Shakira Caine, as well as NBA stars Magic Johnson and Isaiah Thomas, all became Koos fans.

1983 was the year Koos became a U.S. citizen—one of his proudest moments.

Photos on pages 24-25, 26-27 and 28 (left) by Rebecca Blake.

biography (con't)

ut it was the Cosby connection—and those wild, collaged sweaters he wore on TV—that established Koos's reputation with the rich and famous.

More than anyone else, Bill Cosby has been a fan and a friend to Koos, inspiring and supporting him through the good and the lean years. It all began early in the 1980's when Josephine Premice, a beautiful African-American singer, had Koos make a sweater as her present to Bill. Josephine brought the sweater to the set of the Cosby show, where Bill immediately put it on and wore it for the taping. It was an instantaneous hit. Cosby, in his incredibly generous way, began giving his friends presents made by Koos.

…it was the Cosby connection—and those wild, collaged sweaters he wore on TV—that established Koos's reputation with the rich and famous…

Later, Cosby invited some friends to New York for a weekend to celebrate his wife Camille's birthday. He asked Koos to open the store on Sunday, especially for his guests, and told each of them to choose something they liked. Cosby offered the ultimate party favor, while introducing the guests to Koos's designs. Many of the party-goers are still loyal Koos customers.

Soon Koos's designs were everywhere. His clothes dressed stars like Stevie Wonder, Chita Rivera, Brooke Shields, Isabella Rosselini and Lauren Hutton. There was much publicity from the fashion press, including Vogue, Harper's Bazaar and L'Officiel. His clothes were featured in many ads and mailers for Estee Lauder and Virginia Slims cigarettes. He also designed furs for Ben Kahn and sheets for West Point Pepperell, sold at J.C. Penney.

Soon Koos's designs were everywhere.

Once Barbara Walters interviewed Nancy Reagan, and to her embarrassment she and the First Lady both appeared wearing identical Adolfo suits! Ms. Walters' stylist, Sally Sapphire, immediately called Koos to suggest that he design something unique. Ms. Walters subsequently bought a dozen more suits. She sent Koos a photograph of an interview she did with Prime Minister Margaret Thatcher, in which Ms. Walters is wearing a classic white Koos suit. Koos, the inveterate collector and collagist, has incorporated the photo in a wall mural in his store.

After experiencing the highs of the 70's and 80's, a series of events led to a major downturn in Koos's business. He opened the Koos for Men shop on Thompson Street in SoHo, featuring red satin suits, chartreuse pants and chiffon shirts with sequins. After SoHo, another Koos for Men store opened on East 66th Street, just off Madison, in 1986, but was also unsuccessful. Wanting to recapture the trend-setting Madison Avenue woman, Koos had designed an extravagant little boutique, but it didn't work either and the store closed in 1988. Then came the loss of the lease for the 795 Madison Avenue store, when the building was sold in 1990.

Top: The West Village Boutique

Bottom: Inside the present Madison Avenue Boutique.

biography (con't)

In the early 90's, women's tastes were changing and Koos's business was failing. Minimalism was in. Black was in. Collage was out. On top of everything, Koos's business partner was dying. His Madison Avenue lease was cancelled and operations had to be shut down. While the business side of Koos was suffering, his creative vision never faltered. He continued to make garments for his loyal customers.

Then, in 1995, a long-time client, Veronica Vickers, approached Koos with the idea of a new partnership. "Koos & Co." was born. In two short weeks, the business was incorporated, the partners rented a small store on West 10th Street in Greenwich Village, and the renovations started. The little shop in the Village was a success and in 1999, they moved back uptown to 1283 Madison Avenue, between 91st and 92nd Street, where the one and only Koos boutique now stands.

Koos's design philosophy in his own words:

"I think of myself as very basic. I am a craftsperson and I sew like that. I sew beautiful clothes. I am nothing more than a worker sitting behind a sewing machine. That's where I feel most comfortable, that's where I am the best. That's what I do the best and it is very basic."

"I think of myself as very basic. I am a craftsperson and I sew like that. I sew beautiful clothes. I am nothing more than a worker sitting behind a sewing machine. That's where I feel most comfortable, that's where I am the best. That's what I do the best and it is very basic."

koos's studio

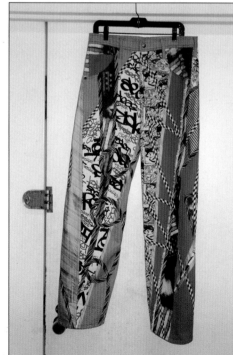

QVC: mass couture

I n 1998, Koos began a new facet of his career. He was introduced to Ellen Alpert, formerly of Saks Fifth Avenue and Harper's Bazaar, and the fashion director for QVC, the home shopping channel. Koos was fascinated by the concept and invited QVC to his workroom.

Ellen proposed that Koos make a small collection of separates and appear on camera behind his sewing machine, to describe how his designs might work for the American lifestyle. The new collection was called "Koos of course!" and sold out in 30 minutes.

"Koos of course!" is an exclusive QVC label and has become their top-selling fashion line, presented monthly. To start the process, Koos creates couture

Koos has aptly named this phenomenal success at QVC "mass couture."

garments, which are interpreted by a manufacturer in the Orient. On the QVC TV program, models wear the mass-produced copies of Koos's boutique originals while Koos and a TV hostess entertain the viewers as orders are taken over the phones. Skirts, blouses, jackets, trousers and sweaters are all under $90. Silks, linens and rayons are used with appliqué and bias tape according to Koos's direction, and with his signature quality and taste.

Koos has aptly named this phenomenal success at QVC "mass couture." He defines it by the numbers—for example, QVC cuts 25,000 jackets for the 68 million people who watch the channel, so 25,000 seems like one-of-a-kind, given the enormous audience.

Koos is extremely proud of his QVC line because it enables him to communicate his design vision to millions of households and to dress women who would not otherwise be able to afford his clothes. He thoroughly enjoys giving fashion advice in his dialogue with the TV call-in customers and continues to be overwhelmed by the sheer magnitude of the American market.

Veronica Vickers, his business partner says, "I think that he senses the customer appreciation which is very gratifying as there are so many of them and it is a positive reinforcement of the service he is providing—Koos fashion at affordable prices. It also validates what he has been doing for the past 35 years in his stores. The power of television has enabled him to reach across the country and talk to the viewer about what he believes in and what personifies his personal sense of style."

… it enables him to communicate his design vision to millions of households…

home sewing

home sewing & quilting

In the winter of 1989 Koos was featured on the cover of *Threads*, with an article that described his work. I was living in Ohio then, and excited to see the feature on Koos and his beautiful clothing. Years later I met the editor of *Threads* at a quilting show and I told her that I had worked for Koos. She enthusiastically informed me that the magazine got its greatest response ever from that article.

Hearing this really inspired me to write a book on Koos's sewing techniques. After years of working for him, I felt that I knew his methods well. But it would take ten years and several transformations of the content until I could work on it diligently.

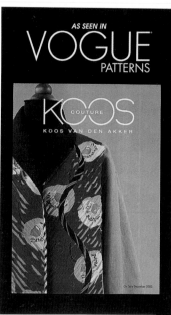

To support the book project, I felt we needed more exposure and stronger marketing. I discovered the perfect promotion—Koos is such a great artist that it just seemed natural for him to design a fabric line.

I approached Kings Road because they produce fabric collections for Laura Heine, another of my authors. Pat Smith, Vice President, was very interested in the work I showed her and understood the cachet of the Koos name and his sophisticated design. We struck a deal and Panorama, the first collection of Koos's fabric, previewed at Fall Quilt Market 2001.

To go along with the fabric line, it seemed logical for Koos to offer some patterns for home sewers to use for their own wearable art. Vogue Patterns in New York City was very familiar with Koos's work and produced two patterns for their Fall/Winter 2002 collections.

In May 2002 at the Spring Quilt Market, Koos had a special exhibit of his work including his new fabric line and Vogue patterns. He sewed in the Kings Road booth, answered questions, and met his many fans.

Koos is such a great artist that it just seemed natural for him to design a fabric line.

*Panorama collection
for Kings Road*

tech

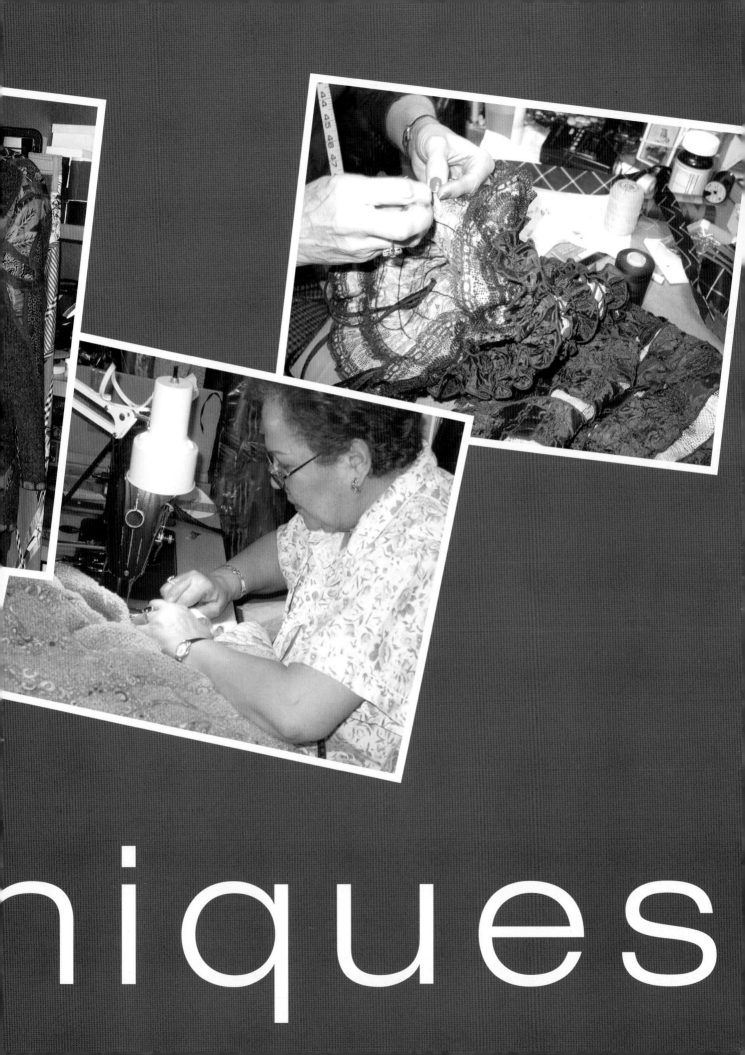

niques

fabric selection

fabric selection

electing the fabrics is the most important factor of the garment and probably the most difficult. While Koos has racks of fabrics in his studio to choose from, the home sewer is more limited.

A suggestion is to start with a background color and pull together fabrics from one color palette and add some coordinating colors as well as a few accent colors. For this gray sweater, there are grays, blacks and olives in the same shade with orange and red accents.

The key to giving the garment visual interest is a variety of textures which means mixing different types of fabrics. To this gray bouclé knit base sweater was added green plaid chiffon, gold and orange plaid taffeta, black leaf rayon brocade, shiny rayon wine and brown check with leather leaf appliqués. The leathers varied also with beige suede, black snake patent, textured olive leather and leopard printed suede.

Any textiles can be used. Look at Home Decorating fabrics or cut up old garments. Koos has even used old fur coats as a base for collage. Scavenge thrift shops for old furs and choose ones with supple skins that aren't dry and brittle.

basic garment style

The essence of a Koos garment is a simple silhouette under the embellishments. One staple is a jacket that closes in the front with a stand-up collar. The body varies as a swing jacket, or with raglan sleeves, or with a zipper closing. This is a great shape to make reversible as Koos often does.

Select a simple shape without many seams to give a nice area for collage.

Give some thought to pre-construction before applying the collage. If side seams are sewn first, the collage can then flow from the front to the back over the seams.

With shoulder seams sewn first, the collage can flow from back to front over the shoulder.

collage design

Koos approaches his collage without anything specific in mind. He generally has the base of the jacket on the table and then rolls out fabric on top and cuts shapes freehand.

This is a bit scary for most home sewers and can use a lot of fabric. An alternative method would be to pre-plan a bit. Either sketch out the collage first on paper or use the newspaper method.

newspaper method

Take different sheets of newspaper including the color comics and place a sheet on top of your fabric base shape. Then either sketch with the marker or try freehand cutting the newspaper. If you like what you see, add another sheet of newspaper and make your second shape. You can move shapes around, eliminate and add more as you like. When you're finished, use the newspaper as a pattern to cut out the actual fabrics.

Look at your collage and check that the lines flow nicely and are not chopped up or intersecting in an odd way. Check the negative shapes to see that they are pleasing and think about where and how you will add bias tape. Select some areas for texturizing such as quilting and slicing. Decide if you will add other surface textures like a tulle or a sheer over a fabric or yarn lines over shapes.

plate method

Another method for collaging would be to make "plates." Cut a rectangle that is big enough to cut out the fronts, backs or sleeves of a jacket and make a collage. Later, place your pattern piece on top and cut it out. These plates can easily be turned into quilts or wall hangings if you choose to later.

Start by using the **Facing Fabric technique** (page 59), then make your collage.

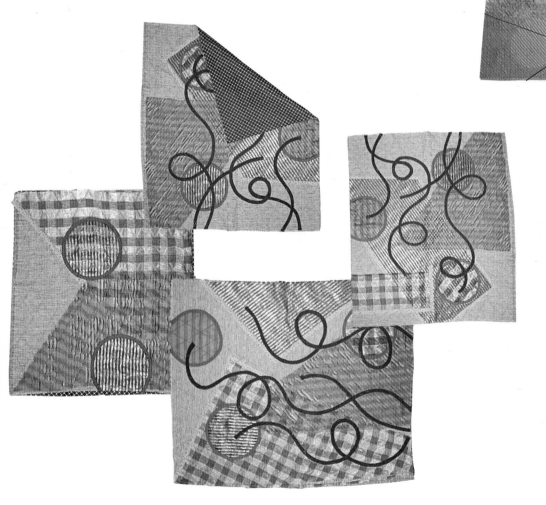

collage design (con't)

After the collage is assembled as desired, spray glue to adhere the pieces to the base cloth. Pins are rarely used, only when textured or thick fabrics won't adhere.

Regular art spray adhesive works but needs to be used in a well-ventilated room. There are many fabric spray adhesives on the market that are more environmentally friendly and safer for the user. They also are spotless and won't gum up the needle.

Carefully pick up the collage piece, place on clean newspaper and spray on wrong side of fabric following directions on can. Replace piece. Press with your hands and smooth out. At this stage you can stitch decorative quilting lines on the applied pieces before adding bias tape

facing fabric

An elegant detail on some of the "unlined" jackets are fabric facings or built-in linings. They give the garment an elegant and couture finish. There are two methods to accomplish this.

yardage method

Lay out the entire outer fabric yardage right side down on the table. Spray the wrong side well with the spray adhesive.

Carefully place the wrong side of a nice "lining" fabric on top of that. It could be the same fabric as a matching blouse, or skirt, or just an accent fabric.

Don't use traditional lining fabrics but rather a layer of a fashion fabric that coordinates in color.

Treat this now as one fabric and cut your pattern pieces out of this yardage of faced fabric.

option:
Cut the yardage into blocks, quilt it and then cut out pattern pieces.

block method

Use this method to individually face each pattern piece.

In this gray coat, the front was cut out and then wrong sides were spray glued to a silk lining.

Cut the lining a few inches larger all around.

When quilted, the lining could shrink in a little. After quilting, trim excess lining even with other layer.

bias tape

bias tape

A distinctive element of Koos's signature style includes bias tape. Bias tape is an integral part of his collage. It's used as a finished edge, as a decorative free-form line or as the outline of an appliquéd piece.

Generally the bias is a woven cotton, silk or rayon 3/8" to 1/2" wide with both long edges turned under (called single fold bias tape).

But Koos also uses other trims in the same way as he uses bias. For example, yarn, lace, thin leather, or ultrasuede strips can be applied in the same manner except where there are tight rounded areas. Bias would be needed for those curves.

There are commercial factories that make custom bias yardage by the spool. Every season Koos selects some good accent or neutral fabrics and sends a few yards of each to be made into bias. He keeps all the rolls together on shelves in his studio so he can see the palette he has to work with.

To create small quantities of bias, Koos uses a simple tool called Bias tapemaker by Clover. It comes in several different widths.

bias tape (con't)

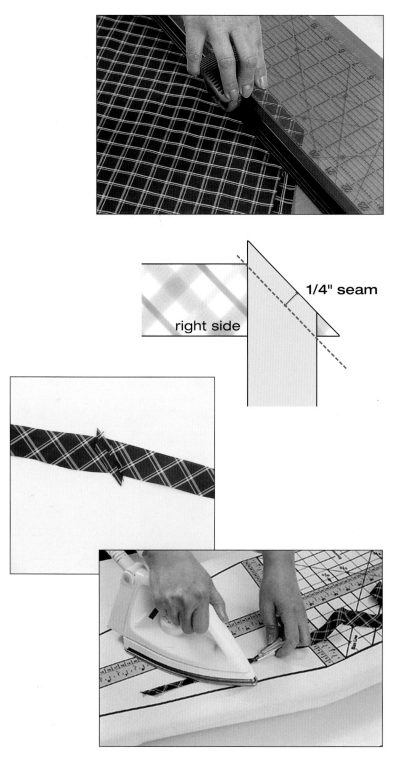

right side

1/4" seam

to make bias tape

1 Cut the fabric into strips diagonally at a 45° angle to the grain.

You must use bias if the tape needs to go around curves.

Using a cutting mat and rotary cutter, place the ruler on the fabric.

For a 1/2" finished tape, cut the fabric strips slightly less than 1" wide.

For a 1" finished tape, cut the fabric strips slightly less than 2" wide.

Also try using the Fiskars all-in-one ruler and rotary cutter (see photo).

2 To join the strips together for a long continuous tape, cut the ends at a 45° angle. Join the strips by placing them right sides together matching the angle as in diagram. Stitch 1/4" seams. Press seam open and flat.

3 To make single-fold bias tape cut one end of the strip at an angle.

Pass the diagonal cut end through the tapemaker and use a pin to help push it through.

Anchor the end of the strip to the ironing board with a pin.

Pull the tapemaker while holding the iron close to the tip.

ultrasuede, leather, suede and vinyl

These materials don't ravel therefore they don't need to have their edges turned under. After they are cut to the desired width, they can be sewn into continuous strips. Because they are not bias, they can only be used for straight lines.

There are many options for the edges of these non-raveling materials.

Fiskars has fancy edge rotary cutter blades that can create beautiful effects.

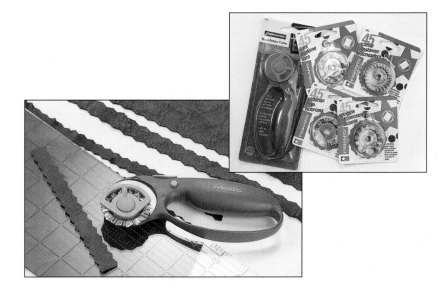

to attach woven bias tape to garment:

Because these strips were cut on the bias, they can be shaped and curved.

For example: To go around a circle, pin the tape around the outer edge first. That edge may stretch slightly and the inner edge will be eased in a little.

After pinning, steam well so bias is flat.

Stitch close to both edges.

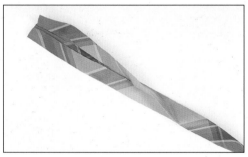

edge binding

1 Make 1" wide single fold bias tape, then fold in half lengthwise and press.

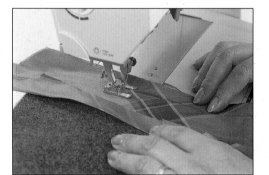

2 Open out one long edge and place cut edge even with wrong side of garment edge. Stitch along first fold line.

3 Fold tape over edge and edge-stitch down on right side of garment.

fabric lace

Using some of the new paper technology on the market, Koos created his own fabric lace. It is used in hems, as inserts and as yardage. This gives an interesting textured sheer look.

supplies:

• YLI Wash-A-Way paper

or

• Mokuba water soluble film

When using YLI water soluble paper for a long or large area, overlap the paper 1/4" and stitch it together first.

hint:

To make narrow fabric strips approximately 1/4" wide, run the fabric through the serger instead of cutting by hand. You could take the needle out but with the needle in, it may gather the fabric and give it texture.

fabric lace (con't)

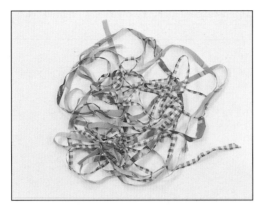

1 Arrange the fabric strips, yarn, and lace on the water soluble paper in a random manner.

2 Place another sheet of paper on the top to hold everything together, or use clear water soluble stabilizer or a piece of sheer fabric. Pin as needed.

3 Stitch through all layers with many rows of stitching, close together either in a grid or in a random pattern. This works best with the "free-motion" technique. Drop the feed-dogs and use a darning foot.

Tulle or lace could also be used as a base—before adding the strips—or on top instead of the clear stabilizer.

When using the Mokuba film, take off the backing to expose the adhesive. Then lay the fabric strips, pieces of scraps, lace, etc. on top and press down to adhere.

Place the clear film on top and stitch.

lace strips

lace strips (con't)

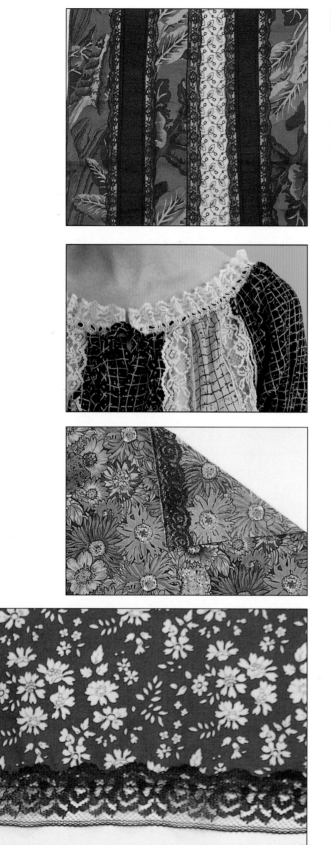

This technique has been used by Koos often throughout the years to create his own fabric. It is a timeless, appealing look that can be used for formal wear, lingerie, peasant blouses and day dresses.

1 Make a block that will be large enough to cut your pattern piece from.

Use straight edges or scalloped edges of any width lace.

2 Cut strips of various fabrics in desired widths. They may vary in the garment.

3 Put the wrong side of the lace on the wrong side of the fabric and stitch 1/4".

4 Press seam flat so 1/4" of lace is on top of right side of fabric.

Trim **fabric only** close to stitching.

Stitch close to lace edge.

When sewing the scalloped edge, measure the 1/4" seam from the closest point (diagram below).

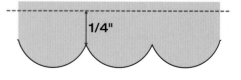

slicing

Slicing is an interesting surface texture that is simple to achieve. Generally it is done with two layers of fabric. The effect gives you a peek of the under-fabric.

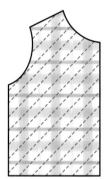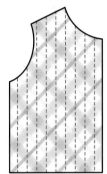

The most important thing to remember is that the actual cutting of the top fabric **must** be on the true bias—45° to the weave. Therefore the stitching must also be on the true bias.

By cutting on the bias, there is usually very little ravel at the edge.

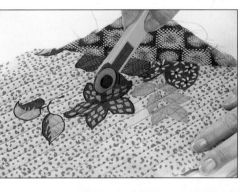

Sew parallel rows of stitching from 1/2" to 1" apart and slice in the center between the stitching, being very careful not to cut the base fabric. Small rounded-tip scissors work well. You can also try the Clover slash cutter which is made to slide between the stitching and cut multi-layers, but not the bottom layer (see photo).

Sometimes steaming will curl back the edges or they can be roughly brushed with your hands.

slicing (con't)

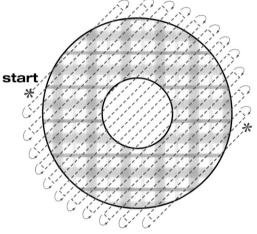

circle slicing

1 Draw circles on your top fabric.

2 Draw lines on bias.

3 Stitch lines 1/2" wide and off the outline, pivot and continue stitching as in diagram.

start

4 Cut between the rows of stitching.

pressed scallop slicing

This example uses two bias layers on top of a backing fabric on the straight grain. Use natural fibers that press well—synthetics will spring back.

1 Stitch on bias about 3/4" apart.

2 Cut top two layers between stitching lines being careful not to cut bottom layer.

3 Stitch perpendicular rows 2" apart.

4 Stretch top two layers to curve and press.

variations

Using a stretch knit base add a top layer of woven fabric. Stitch parallel lines and slice for a t-shirt.

Try using a knit on top and stretch it slightly before stitching. When cut, it will pull back and show the bottom layer.

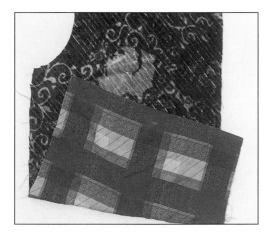

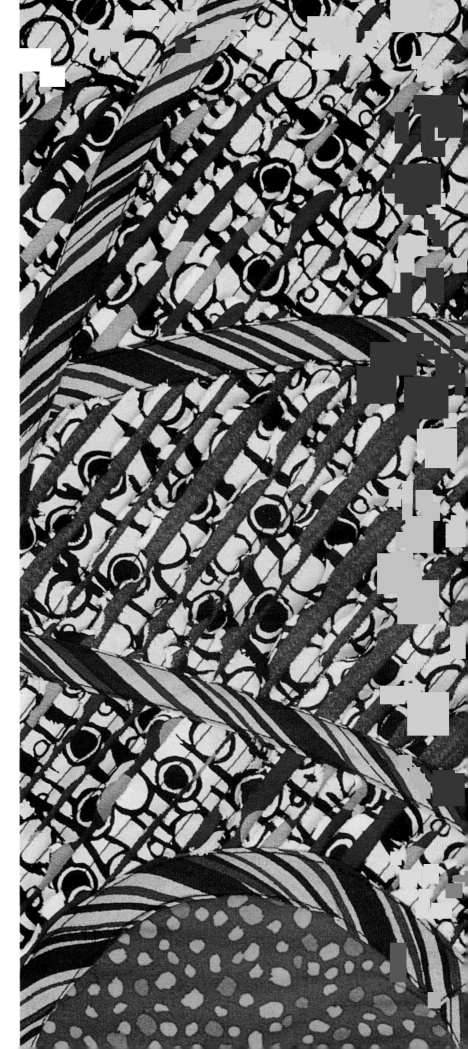

yarn trim

Yarn is used here artfully to outline or as a "drawing" element.

Couch over the yarn using either a matching thread or clear nylon invisible thread and the zig-zag stitch.

Or, use a special presser foot that will guide the yarn in the center and straight-stitch right in the center of the yarn.

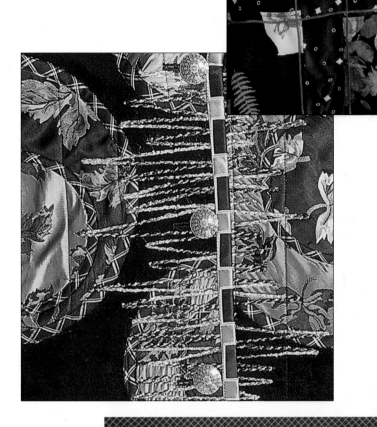

origami patch

origami patch

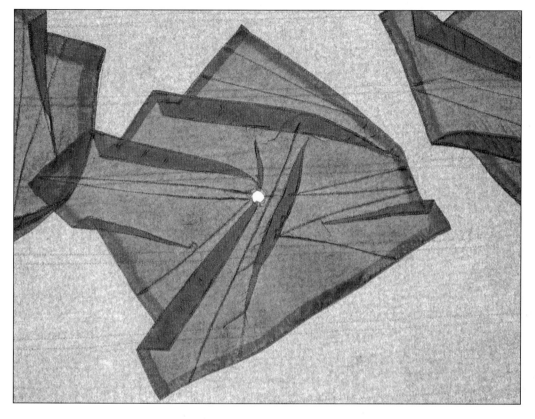

The fabric for the Origami patch should be a natural fiber that creases well. In this coat black silk organza is used.

1 Visually estimate the size and number of patches desired.

Cut size of patch 1" larger all around. Don't draw the patch exactly—just rough cut a square or rectangle.

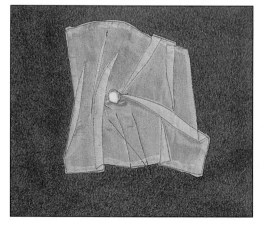

2 On front of the coat, place a pin through where the center hole will be and mark on the wrong side.

Place center of patch on back, pin and draw a small circle on the patch approx 1/2" diameter.

Using a small stitch length, sew around the circle.

3 Snip away inside circle close to stitching.

Push the fabric through the hole to the right side.

Press under 1/4" to 3/8" roughly on all four sides of patch.

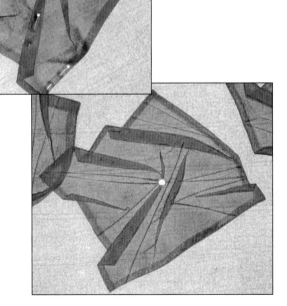

4 Fold creases into patch and pin. When you have it as desired, press the creases flat.

5 Edgestitch around the outer edges of creases and then the long edges of creases through the middle and around the center hole.

6 Add extra stitching lines on the flat areas for more detail as desired.

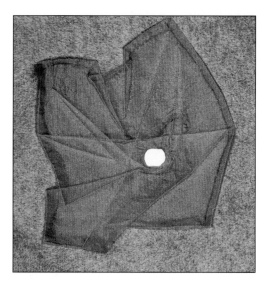

origami patch variations

- Origami buttonhole of leather (see page 98).

- Patch edges serged and strings hanging (page 98).

- Patch on front with no hole and appliqué detail (see photo bottom right).

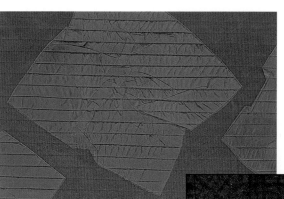

Oh! I see ~~but~~ WHAT YOU W IS LOVE.

image transfer

You can transfer any flat image onto fabric. The transfer paper method works best on tightly woven fabrics: silks, cotton, polyester, flat wool and sheers.

For this shirt, Koos first transferred a child's drawing onto cotton. Then it was cut to fit the shirt pattern piece.

supplies:

- Dragon Threads image transfer paper
- Use of a color laser copier

There are significant differences between using a color laser copier versus a home computer printer. The laser copier will transfer an image exactly the same as the original with excellent color and sharpness. Also the image will not fade when machine washed or dried and gets softer with repeated washings.

The home computer color printer uses different inks and most will wash out or fade, sometimes even after a fixative is applied.

1 Put the image transfer paper in the paper drawer of the copier with the back printed side facing up. Close the drawer.

2 Place the image on the copier glass. Select "mirror image" if there is any writing in the photos. Otherwise, the image/wording will come out in reverse on the fabric.

You can also enlarge or reduce the image at this stage.

Press the "print" button.

3 Trim most of the white margins from the paper.

4 The iron should be at the hottest temperature without steam. Let the iron warm up for about 10 minutes. Be careful that it doesn't shut off and cool down if it's the automatic shut-off type.

5 Iron all wrinkles out of the fabric and brush away any lint. With warm fabric, place the transfer, image side down, on the fabric.

6 Place fabric on a hard surface (not an ironing board). Press **very** firmly and hold the iron in place for 15 seconds. Move iron to another area and press firmly for 15 seconds.

Move the iron around until the entire picture is heated up. Then peel the paper off immediately even though it's hot to the touch. The paper should peel off cleanly.

note:
It's always best to test fabric and temperature first on scrap fabric.

ruffles & self trim

Strips of fabric can be used to embellish garments. The strips can be cut using a rotary cutter and mat or with the aid of a serger.

Run fabric through the serger using the guide to the right of the cutter to "cut" the fabric into strips of desired width. It's very fast and easy.

For the gathered or pleated ruffle, first serge both long edges.

In the green jacket, the raw edges were left unfinished and were slightly ravelled.

appliqué

appliqué

otifs from fabric prints can be used as appliqués. You can trace a shape from fabric, leather or another material.

When Koos finds a shape he likes, he cuts it from cardboard and uses it often as an appliqué element.

Here you see some favorite cardboard templates hanging on the wall of his studio (photo top right).

appliqué (con't)

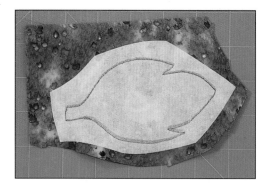

1 Trace your design onto the paper side of Steam-A-Seam. Remember that it will be a mirror image when cut from fabric.

2 Cut roughly around the paper. Peel off backing and stick the shape onto the fabric.

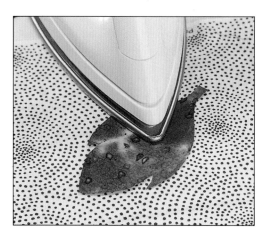

3 Cut shape exactly on the lines. Peel off remaining paper backing.

4. Place shape on base in position and iron with medium-high iron. Press down rather than sliding the iron back and forth.

5 Sometimes Koos doesn't stitch the appliqué down, but when he does he usually just stitches close to the raw edges. The edges won't ravel because they are fused.

finishing

Many of Koos's garments are reversible or clean finished on the inside because they are usually unlined. See Facing Fabrics (page 59) because this is done first.

Following are some methods Koos uses for a clean finish.

flat felled seam

1 With right sides together, sew seam.

2 Trim one side to 1/4".

3 Take untrimmed side and press under long edge.

4 Press this side over to cover the narrow edge and edgestitch.

option:
Narrow serge long untrimmed edge and then press under.

bias tape seam

1 Sew a regular seam.

2 Trim both seam allowances to 1/4".

3 Press seam open and flat.

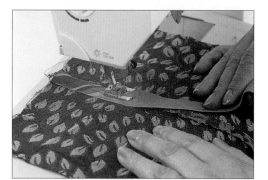

4 Apply wider 5/8"–3/4" bias over both seams to cover and stitch close to both edges.

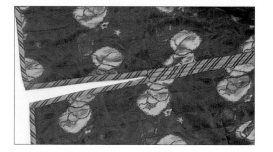

bound seams

1 Bind the edges with a narrow bias tape approximately 1/2" flat (see Bias tape/Edge binding, page 64).

2 Sew seam with wrong sides together so seam is on the outside of the garment.

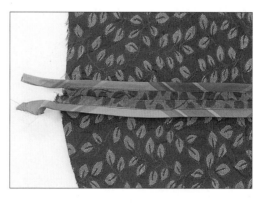

3 Press the seam open and stitch flat through the bias close to the fold edge.

note:
On the blue jacket above, the sleeve cap was attached first and then the underarm and side seam were done in one long bound seam.

origami buttonhole

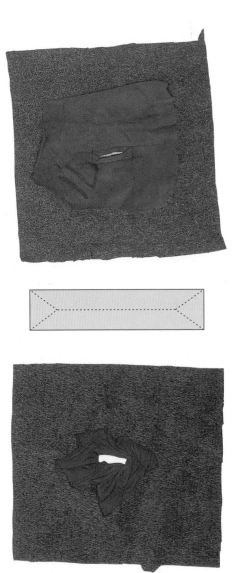

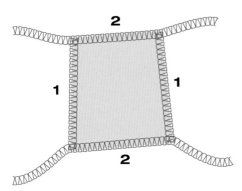

for leather or suede

1 Cut odd shape patch bigger than button. Thin leather works best.

2 Place right side leather to wrong side fabric.

3 Mark buttonhole. Stitch bound buttonhole rectangle appropriate size to fit button. This is automatic on most high-end machines.

4 Cut out ⟩⟨ shape (diagram left).

5 Push leather through to front side. Smooth around opening and press wrinkles into leather and spray glue down.

6 Irregularly sew down leather.

for raveling fabric

First fuse your raveling fabric to Steam-A-Seam 2 Light. Then use as above. When you crease your fabrics and stitch, the raw edge should be secure and not ravel when cleaned or:

1 Cut irregular rectangular patch.

2 Narrow serge opposite sides. Then serge remaining sides leaving long tails at the beginning and end (diagram left).

3 Continue with Step 2 above.

> **note:**
> This technique can also be used with larger openings for pockets.

hong kong edge

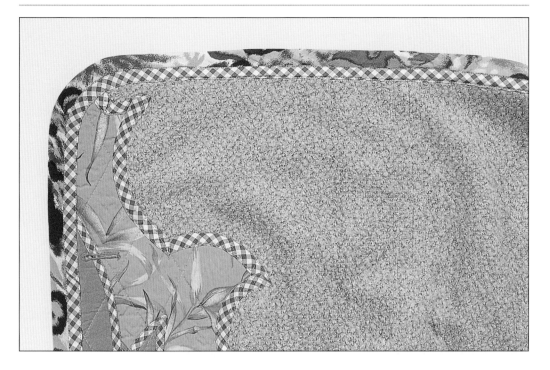

1 Cut bias strip (pink floral silk)
2" wide.

2 Sew right side of the bias to
wrong side of garment using
1/2" seam.

3 Fold over edge to front of
jacket and stitch 1/4" away from
previous stitching, or 3/4" from
edge of jacket.

4 Trim this raw edge close to the
stitching.

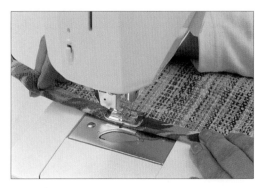

5 Apply narrow single fold bias
(check) to cover raw edge of
floral silk.

6 To join at the end, fold under
edge a scant 1/4" and overlap.

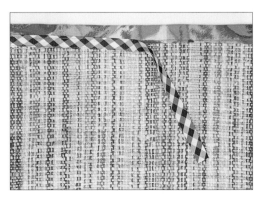

origami jacket details

Jacket faced in printed silk

6" strip of black silk taffeta for cuff turnback

Assymetrical placement of patches

cashmere circle jacket details

Look for unusual fabrics for bias tape. These squares are woven on the bias.

Black cashmere faced with printed and flocked chiffon

spiral sleeve seam

Sew together a raglan sleeve pattern out of muslin. With marker, draw desired spiral seam line. Try on to see how it looks. Cut along line and lay muslin flat. Trace to make a paper pattern and add 5/8" seam along the cut line. Place cording in center of wide bias strip and use zipper foot to stitch close to cording. Insert into seam.

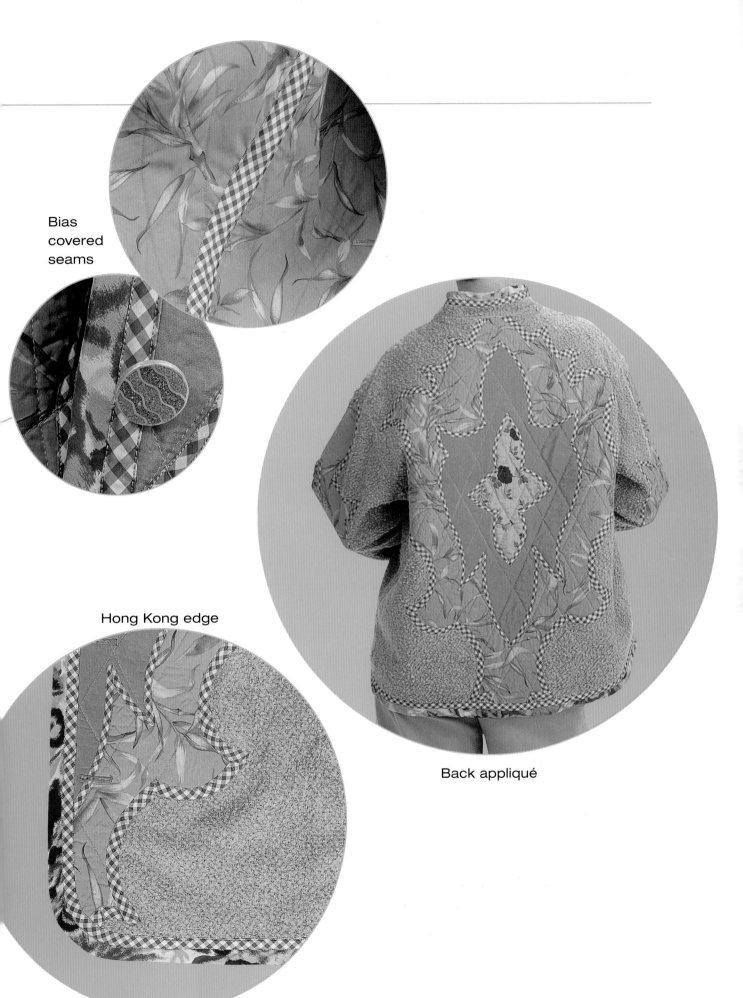

Bias
covered
seams

Hong Kong edge

Back appliqué

leaf sweater details

Sleeve

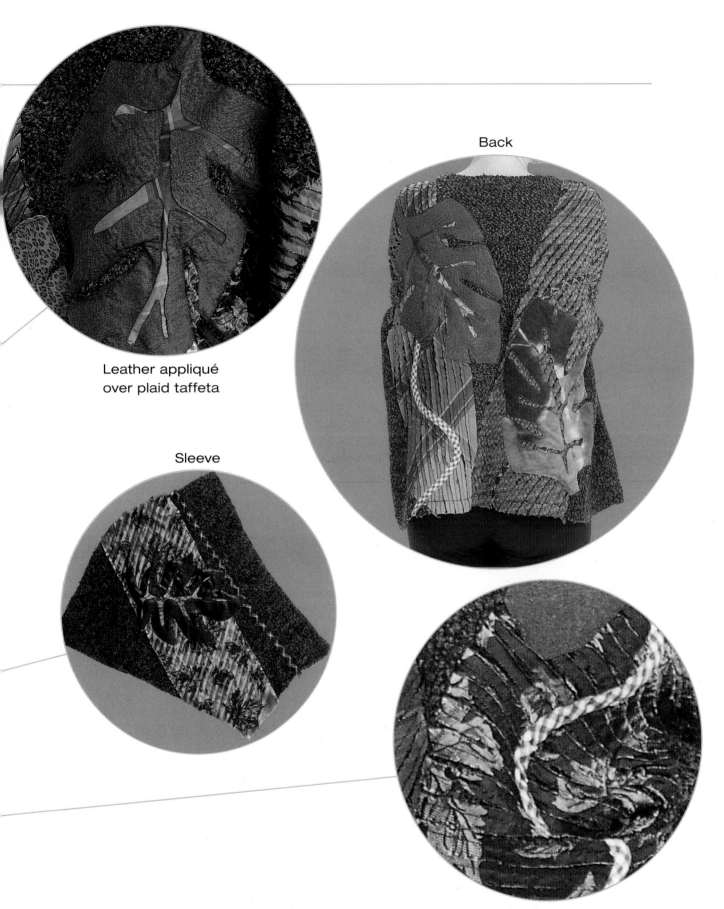

Leather appliqué
over plaid taffeta

Back

Sleeve

Slicing and
applied bias tape

Atelier Marketing Group Ltd.
Licensing agent for Koos
490 Tucker Drive
Worthington, OH 43085
614-841-9388, fax 614-841-9389

Babylock
sewing machines
1760 Gilsinn Lane
Fenton, MO 63026
For a dealer near you call:
800-482-2669
www.babylock.com

Bernina
sewing machines
3500 Thayer Ct.
Aurora, IL 60504
For a dealer near you call:
800-877-0477
www.berninausa.com

Rebecca Blake
photographer
contact: lostangel@rcn.com

Clover
slash cutter, bias tape makers
1007 E. Dominguez St.
Carson, CA 90746
800-233-1703

Dragon Threads
image transfer paper, sewing books,
sewing notecards,
490 Tucker Drive
Worthington, OH 43085
614-841-9388, fax 614-841-9389
www.dragonthreads.com

Elna
sewing machines
1760 Gilsinn Lane
Fenton, MO 63026
For a dealer near you call:
800-848-ELNA
www.elnausa.com

Fairfield Processing
batting
88 Rose Hill Ave.
Danbury, CT 06810
800-980-8000

Fiskars
scissors, rotary cutter, mats, rotary
cutter/ruler, fancy cutting blades
Box 8027
Wausau, WI 54402
800-950-0203
www.fiskars.com

Karter Bias & Trimming
45" fabric—minimum 3 yds—$30
(1 yd = 84 yds of 1/2" bias.)
Brooklyn Army Terminal & 58th St.,
Brooklyn, NY 11220
718-745-6664, ask for Nelson

Kings Road Imports
Koos's fabric lines.
548 S. Los Angeles St.
Los Angeles, CA 90013
For a store near you call:
800-433-1546
www.kingsrd.com

Koos Boutique
1283 Madison Ave. (91st St.)
NY, NY 10128
212-722-9855

Leather Suede Skins Inc.
261 West 35 Street, 11th floor
NY, NY 10001
212-967-6616
www.leathersuedeskins.com

Mokuba
water soluble paper, ribbons
55 West 39 St.,
NYC, NY 10018
212-869-8900

OESD
spray adhesive, threads
1-800-580-8885
www.oesd.com

QVC
Koos of Course! garments
800-345-1515
www.qvc.com

Robison-Anton
threads
Box 159,
Fairview, NJ 07022
www.robisonanton.com

Rowenta
irons, steam generator
For a dealer near you call:
1-800-rowenta
www.rowentausa.com

Sulky
threads, stabilizers,
spray adhesive
water soluble paper,
3113 Broadpoint Dr
Harbor Heights, FL 33983
800-874-4115
www.sulky.com

Superior Threads
800-499-1777
www.superiorthreads.com

The Warm Company
Steam-A-Seam 2
954 E. Union St.
Seattle, WA 98122
800-234-9276
www.warmcompany.com

YLI
water soluble paper, threads
161 West Main St.
Rock Hill, SC 29730
800-836-8139
www.ylicorp.com

bibliography

Round Bobbin Club News
Summer 2002

Women's Wear Daily
May 29, 2002

Sewing Professional
September 2002

Quilting Professional
May 2002

New York Times
Home Design Magazine
April 14, 2002
"Fashion Takes a Seat"
pp. 28-30

New York Times Magazine
January 2002

Los Angeles Times
Jan. 4, 2002
"A Comeback of Vintage Collage"

Vogue
December 2001
"Koos and Effect"
page 191

Threads
Dec. 1989/Jan 1990,
"Koos, the Master of Collage"
by David Page Coffin
pp. 28-33
Taunton Press

Woman's Day
Review for Knitting

The St. James
Fashion Encyclopedia
Richard Martin
pp.392-393
Visible Ink Press, 1997,
Detroit MI

The Thames and Hudson
Dictionary of Fashion and
Fashion Designers
Georgia Callan
p. 246
Thames and Hudson, 1998,
NYC

Linda Chang Teufel has an extensive fashion background. She received her Bachelor of Fine Arts degree in Fashion Design from Pratt Institute where she apprenticed for Koos in her senior year.

After receiving her degree, she worked in the New York fashion design industry for a textile firm, Cathy Hardwick and Koos. She held positions in fashion retailing and merchandising for Macy's New York and Victoria's Secret Catalogue.

In 1987, she moved to Columbus, Ohio and attended The Ohio State University for a teaching certificate in Home Economics Education. After the birth of her first son, she wrote and published her first book, *Fabric Origami*, and started teaching across the country on the sewing circuit.

Linda is the founder of the publishing company Dragon Threads and has published several books by other sewing and quilting specialists. Linda has written several articles for most of the major sewing and quilting magazines and has designed several embroidery cards. Through the years she has taught for many of the sewing machine companies, International Quilt Festival, American Sewing Guild, sewing machine dealers and numerous private guilds and conferences.

Linda lives in Worthington, Ohio with her husband and two sons.

Koos's friends,
1983,
New York City